Advice from a Publisher

(Insider Tips for Getting Published)

Lacey L. Bakker

Pandamonium Publishing House

www.pandamoniumpublishing.com

Cover Design: Alex Goubar

ISBN: 9781989506141

DEDICATION

To every writer who has something to say and
wants their words to outlive them.

CONTENTS

INTRODUCTION

I decided to write this book because of a need in the marketplace. Not many publishers are willing to offer insider tips to help up and coming authors with the publishing process. In fact, most publishers send out nothing more than form rejection letters with no help or suggestions for improving the author's chances of getting a book deal. As a publisher and author, I'm spilling the secrets on what publishers want and what no one in the industry will tell you! You can find out more about me at the end of this book in the About the Author Section on page 54.

1
TO SELF-PUBLISH OR TRADITIONAL PUBLISH? THAT IS THE QUESTION

When I first started out as a writer, I had enough rejection slips to wallpaper the side of my house. I still have all of them in a box in my office to remind me how far I've come since my early days of submitting my work to traditional publishers.

Eventually, my writing improved, and I broke through the barrier that stood between me and becoming a traditionally published author. After being published internationally over a dozen times and writing for various publications, I decided that I wanted to try the process of self-publishing a children's book. I had done a lot of research on the process and decided that I wanted to earn a higher royalty, be in complete creative control of the book from beginning to end, and I wanted to learn everything I could about the self-publishing space while I was at it.

I have an educational background in marketing and

advertising as well as children's literature and publishing. Having a business background was about to help me more that I could have ever imagined during my eventual publishing career! We'll talk more about my story throughout this book, but for now, let me help you make the best choice for *your* work by explaining the differences between self-publishing and traditional publishing.

There are a lot of differences between self-publishing and traditional publishing. Let's start off with definitions for each:

Self -Publishing is the publication or creation of a written work that has no involvement from an established publisher. Self-publishing means that the author is responsible for the entire process of publication from conception to marketing and everything in between. This includes, but is not limited to, formatting, design, cover creation, marketing, selling, and obtaining the ISBN (International Standard Book Number). The author is also responsible for all costs surrounding the publication of their work, as well as reporting all earnings to the government as required. The author and creator of the work is additionally responsible for formatting their book into digital versions if so desired. Of course, the author could hire professionals such as graphic designers and formatters to help with the design process. The creator of the work would be responsible for finding a printer and for getting distribution of their book.

As you can see, self-publishing can be a long and arduous process, especially for first timers. There are publishing companies that assist self-published authors with the processes surrounding the publications of their work. For example, at our company, Pandamonium Publishing House, we put the author in touch with our stable of graphic designers, formatters, and editors. Yes, self-publishing is a bit of a learning curve, but once you get the hang of it, it becomes much easier.

Traditional Publishing is when a publisher or publishing house signs an agreement with an author to buy their work. The publisher is responsible for turning the manuscript into a book and paying the author a royalty. The publisher oversees all the details from editing to the final product and everything in between; they are the ones who have the final say and can make any necessary changes as they see fit. A publisher's job is to make sure the book is saleable. Publishing is a business and businesses need to profit in order to continue.

Sometimes there are advances given to authors that go against future sales. For example, a publisher buys a manuscript from an author at a cost of $5,000, this is called an advance. Then the book goes on to sell $5,000 worth of copies. The author is paid no more than that amount, they've already been given their money IN ADVANCE. If the book sells $10,000 worth of copies, the author is paid the $5,000 advance, and then a percentage of retail sales or around 50 cents per copy sold afterward. Traditional publishing is taking a risk on an author who is unknown. Some traditional publishers do not pay advances to their authors, but they pay a higher royalty rate for each retail sale. This can be anywhere from $1 per book to $1.50 per book depending on the House.

Self-publishing *can* be more lucrative after the initial

investment because you get to keep the profits and the creative control. I don't suggest this method to everyone because it's extremely involved and without any type of business or marketing background, it can be a struggle. Did you know that most self-published authors never sell more than 100 copies of their book? That's why it's important to team up with a publisher that offers help with self-publishing services rather than go at it alone.

Pros of Self-Publishing:

1) **Creative control of the project from beginning to end.** You get to choose the cover design, editing process and changes to your manuscript, the sizing of your book, page count, layout, formatting process, the printer you use, how many copies of your book you print, sales, distribution, the price you set for your book, and marketing.

2) **Higher royalty rate.** When you choose to self-publish you get to keep more money. As I stated previously, there is an initial investment on your part to publish your book, but after costs, you get to keep the profit. Plus, once you get enough sales under your belt to cover the initial investment, the rest is profit in your pocket. Some of our royalty rates are 80% of retail sales for the self-published titles at Pandamonium Publishing House. Also, you can charge whatever you'd like for appearance fees such as school visits or lectures for example.

3) **You're in charge.** You get to set your fees and your schedule, you chose the events that you participate in, you decide when and where you'd like to do book signings, when you post on social media, and how you engage with your audience. This is your baby

and you can nurture it any way you choose. You get to do whatever you want to do to sell your book.

4) **Tax write-offs.** By no means am I a tax guru so please seek advice from your accountant with this. If you set up your self-published book as a business or a publishing company, you can choose between a sole-proprietorship or corporation to report your taxes. Write-offs include things such as a percentage of mileage for events to sell your book at, a portion of your home office, office supplies, and a whole host of other things.

5) **Continuing education**. If you choose to further your career as a writer (which I highly recommend), you'll need to take as many continuing education classes as you can. Writing is something that needs to be improved upon constantly especially when choosing to write in new genres. Classes, seminars, workshops, and lectures are all part of continuing education and sometimes these events are held abroad. As a self-published author, you can decide where you'd like to learn more about your craft and if you'd like to travel. I've been to Toronto, London England, New York, Boston, Pittsburgh, Florida, and the Cayman Islands for writers retreats and classes. Not only are these events educational, but they're fun and can lead to friendships that last a lifetime.

Cons of Self-Publishing:

1) **The initial and ongoing investment**. Self-publishing can cost anywhere from $5,000 and upwards of $10,000. Plus, there are ongoing expenses. If you don't have the money to invest

upfront, you could raise money through crowdfunding, loans, investments from friends and family, or by doing things in stages as your budget allows. The initial investment is to take your book from conception to completion and the ongoing investment is printing costs, marketing, and inventory. Additionally, when you write one book, it's rare that you'll never write another!

2) **Wearing too many hats**. You are the person in charge of everything as mentioned before. You'll be the one answering emails, interviewing illustrators/cover designers, you're the marketing and sales team, and social media guru. You're the shipper and receiver and the person responsible for ordering inventory and maintaining your sales site. There are quite honestly at least fifty jobs that you do while self-publishing. Of course, you could hire help, but most times there's not enough left in the budget, so you end up doing things yourself to save money. This is not only time consuming, but counterproductive. The old adage, jack of all trades master of none, comes to mind.

3) **Finding the right people**. You'll need contacts for bookstores and signings, graphic artists, illustrators, formatter, printer, and an editor. You'll need a group of beta readers, people who will give you honest reviews, and you must find the right people to get in front of for distribution of your book. How can people read your work if they don't know where to find it? Plus, if you're shy or skew toward the introverted side of the personality scale, this will be difficult for you. You're going to have to knock on a ton of doors and a lot of those doors will be slammed in your face. YOU must be the right type

of person to take the rejection that comes with self-publishing as it's not for the faint of heart or easily discouraged.

4) **Sales.** The amount of money you make with your self-published book is entirely up to you. You choose the price point, but you are also responsible for all sales. How much should you charge for your book? How do you take payments? How do you charge tax? Do you know how much tax to charge? What about bulk sales and discounts on orders? How will you process returns or damages? Where will you sell your book and which platforms will you use? The best advice I've ever received in my entire career was this, "While writing a book, it's an art. When the book is completed, it's a business; never confuse the two."

5) **Marketing.** You need to print business cards and signage, plus you'll need feature sheets and postcards. There will be mailouts and press releases that need to be designed and you'll need to create a website. Being responsible for all these things is time consuming and can be quite expensive. Plus, if you don't have a marketing background, the book business can eat you alive because it gets complicated.

If you're not ready to deal with the cons of self-publishing, then you're not ready to publish your own book without the help of self-publishing professionals. When you purchase a package from Pandamonium Publishing House, we're right beside you every step of the way. We ensure that all of the above *and more* gets done. Plus, we know the right people to connect you with in every area of your project.

Now that we've talked about the pros and cons of self-publishing, let's explore the pros and cons of traditional publishing.

Pros of Traditional Publishing:

1) **You get paid for your work.** The publisher purchases your work and pays you an advance and/or royalty. All you have to do is write the book and complete the revisions that the editor expects. Plus, you will receive a royalty on your book for the life of the work.
2) **Everything is handled.** From your marketing plan to publicity and book signings, the publisher handles it all. They tell you where to be and when. They take care of you and your book from beginning to end. There's nothing that you have to do except write the book, show up, and engage with your readers. Plus, they handle all of the sales, payments, earning reports, and inventory as well as the editing, design, formatting, and creation of your book.
3) **Opportunity.** Publishers have a vast network of contacts and from those contacts comes opportunity. Your book and your face will be in front of a ton of people and media personnel. You'll be given opportunities that most people only dream of. My authors have appeared on documentary series', in newspapers, on radio shows, featured on blogs around the world, interviewed on internet segments, YouTube channels, podcasts, and on red carpets.

Cons of Traditional Publishing:

1) **You have no control**. The publisher is in total control of your manuscript and your book. They choose the parts they want cut or extended, they hire the cover designer and ensure that the book looks the way it needs to whether you like the cover or not. Publishers turn the manuscript into something saleable because publishing is a business and your book is a product.

2) **Expectations are high**. The industry is changing, and publishers now rely on authors to do their part. Not only do we expect authors to engage with their readers at book signings and events, we ask them to be active on social media and have an author platform in place before the book is published. We also expect them to promote their books on various platforms such as live readings on YouTube and Facebook. We also set a minimum sales target for their book to have a reprint, if it doesn't reach the threshold, we don't do another print run.

3) **No guarantees**. You may not get a reprint of your current book (this is dependent on your contract and of course, sales) or another publishing deal even if we've published you before. Things change all the time and new authors and ideas come on the scene. There are no guarantees in life and especially no guarantees in publishing.

Another thing we should touch on is the stigma (which is thankfully lessening) around self-published books; some people feel that self-publishing is "cheating" or "vanity publishing" or that the author couldn't get anyone to publish them because their work wasn't good enough. This isn't the case. People self-publish for a variety of reasons and just because you made a book yourself, doesn't discount your title as a "real" author.

Self-publishing is a business and if you remember that and put out a top-quality product, you'll be able to compete in the marketplace. I encourage self-publishing when it's done properly and with the right amount of knowledge and discipline.

Insider Secret: Try your hand at self-publishing an e-book to see if you can handle the process; you'll be able to do it for little cost other than the investment of your time. You can do this on Amazon quickly and easily! Print books are more advanced and require more steps, but if you're successful and comfortable after self-publishing an e-book, that knowledge can help take the fear out of publishing a print book!

2
HOW TO PROPERLY QUERY

Query letters are essential! Not enough importance from potential authors is placed on query letter mastery. The point of a query letter to a publisher is to get the publisher to ask for more pages of your manuscript to be submitted. Good query letters whet our appetite and pique our interest, bad queries make us cringe and move onto the next one. Query letters are your chance to sell the publisher or agent on your manuscript and it should offer the saleable aspects of your work. Your manuscript is for sale, start enticing us to buy!

Query letters are sent usually via an online portal, or by a dedicated submission page, or via email. Very rarely do publishers receive any part of the submission process by snail mail since the introduction of the internet and email.

There are 4 parts to a query letter, let's dig in:

1) **Title, Word Count, Genre, and Category**. What is the name of your book (even a working title is fine)?

What is the word count? E.g. 80,000 words. What is the genre? E.g. Romantic Fiction. What is the Category? E.g. Cozy Romance

2) **Description of your story and the HOOK.** The hook is what gets us, well, hooked! What does your character want? Why do they want it? And who or what keeps them from getting it? INCLUDE THE ENDING!

3) **A bit about yourself.** We want to know you! What writing credentials do you have? Have you won any awards or attended any classes for continuing education? Have we met you at a conference before? Etc.

4) **Thank you and closing line.** E.g. Thank you for reading my submission and I look forward to your response. Quick, easy, and cuts to the chase.

The query letter **should not** be longer than one page. Get to the point, why should we request more information about you and your book?

DO NOT put this in your query letter:

1) **That friends and family love your book.** Let us be the judge, it's our job to be objective and we know what the market wants.

2) **How many times you've been rejected.** This is irrelevant and does not make us feel sorry for you.

3) **How much money you've spent** on an editor/stamps/printing manuscripts. This makes you sound like you're complaining. Plus, we pay for an editor anyways and we only expect a pretty good polished version, but not perfection at this point.

4) **That you're the next** *insert famous author name here* or the *next NYTimes Bestseller.* This makes you sound arrogant, desperate, and out of touch.

Insider Secret: Check out the sample query letter in chapter 7 of this book. Also, address your query specifically to the person you want to read it. E.g. Attn: Ms. Bakker. Tell the publisher the reason why you chose their House to submit to and be sure to mention if you've met them before at a conference or continuing education summit. If you don't have any writing credentials, it's ok, but don't make them up to sound important or more advanced. If you're self-published, only mention this if you've had astronomical sales of more than 5,000 copies of your book.

Want to join our mini course on crafting the perfect query? Check it out by clicking on the link or by copying and pasting into your browser:

https://pandamoniumpublishing.com/product/mini-course-crafting-the-perfect-query/

3
HOW TO WRITE A SYNOPSIS

Do you want to know what will make a publisher absolutely lose their mind and throw their laptop onto their front lawn? Read on to find out. No, I don't mean read on to find out, I mean when authors say, "Read the book to find out!" Let me explain:

The job of a synopsis is to tell the publisher what happens in your book from beginning to end. It's a snippet of the big picture and gives us the information that we need to know. If you remember from the previous chapter, How to Properly Query, you'll know that a query letter is a *sales pitch*. A synopsis is an *overview of your book* which allows the publisher to identify any major problems with your manuscript, let's us determine if your book is a good fit, and helps us decide if your work is exciting, intriguing, and fresh enough to publish.

Your synopsis must include:

1) **The main character and why we should care about them.** What is at stake and what motivates this character to take action?
2) **The conflict.** How does the main character succeed or fail in dealing with the conflict?
3) **Conflict resolution?** How is the conflict resolved and has the character changed or learned anything? THIS IS THE ENDING! DO NOT PUT *READ ON TO FIND OUT* because your letter will be recycled, and you'll never hear from us again. Seriously, this drives us crazy.

DO NOT:

1) **Summarize each scene or every chapter.** This will take way too long, and you must get your summary across quickly and concisely.
2) **Write this with the tone of a book jacket or back cover.** It's not a marketing piece for readers that builds excitement.
3) **Make your synopsis longer than one page.**
4) **Get weighed down with specifics** such as supporting character names, detailed settings, and descriptions.
5) **Talk about character back story.** We don't need to know and frankly we don't care. Yes, even for you sci-fi writers, leave it out!
6) **Get wordy.** Don't use eight words when four will do.

For examples of good and bad synopsis' check out chapter 7.

Insider Secret: Write your synopsis in the third person narrative even if your manuscript is told in first person. Write in the present tense and remind the publisher of the category and genre of your work. Reveal EVERYTHING and never use, *it was all a dream* endings or beginnings.

4
SUBMISSION GUIDELINES

I receive up to one hundred and fifty manuscript submissions per month during our busy season which is from September to December. On average I can count on sixty submissions per month to come across my desk. Half of all submissions are not done properly which automatically excludes those potential authors from not only from getting a book deal, but from me even reading their submission; the ones who do not follow the guidelines, their work gets recycled immediately.

The reason why submission guidelines are so important are for two reasons:

1) **They show us (publishers) that you as a potential author/client can follow instructions.** We can't work with people who can't follow guidelines because that's what the entire process is based on from beginning to end. If you aren't able to follow a set of simple steps to submission, how in the world are you ever going to do the harder things

that need to be done such as complete deadlines, revisions, and take advice. Not doing this process shows us that you're not invested enough in doing things correctly or systematically.

2) **It allows publishers to do their job more efficiently.** We don't want to be searching for information because we don't have time or the desire to do so. Publishers have a set of guidelines in place because this allows us to find the information we need quickly. Time is not our friend and with all the submissions we receive, you make our job easier if you follow the guidelines. You make our job easier if you don't follow the guidelines as well, because we know that we don't even have to read what you've sent, and your submission will be trashed immediately.

Every publisher has their own specific set of guidelines which can be found on their site. They are usually under the *about us* tab or will have a dedicated section for submission questions. Guidelines can vary depending on the type of books the publisher is looking for and what they publish. For example, novel submission guidelines vary from that of children's book guidelines. Magazines and other kinds of publications have different expectations and a quick Google search will help you find out exactly what you need to do, plus the stipulations for each.

Ours can be found at:
https://pandamoniumpublishing.com/about/

Some common guidelines include:

1) **Query** (See chapter 2 of this book)
2) **Synopsis** (See chapter 3 of this book)
3) **The first 5-10 pages** pasted in the body of the email. Publishers rarely, if ever, open attachments from unknown sources.
4) What to put in the **subject line** to ensure that it reaches the right person or department of the company/ who to submit your work to.
5) Novels must be **completed**, no incomplete works
6) No previously published works
7) Must be **original works** (no fanfiction)
8) **Simultaneous submissions** or exclusive submissions
9) Submissions from a **literary agent** only

When submitting to various houses, follow the rules or risk disqualifying yourself. Some houses require exclusive submissions which means you cannot submit your work to two places at once. No previously published works means that if your book or story has been published before in any capacity (including online) it is rendered inadmissible.

The submission guideline section of the publisher's website will often tell you what type of books they publish and what they are currently looking for. For example, as I'm writing this, Pandamonium Publishing House is looking for middle-grade adventure novels.

Insider Secret: Find out everything you can about the publisher that you're submitting to so that you can tailor your approach specifically to them .Use the information about them online to your advantage, and address the person in charge by name, respectfully. Look at their products and see where your book would fit best and be sure to mention this in your query. Mention a few things about their company that you appreciate or noticed and put it in your query letter. This simple action impresses us, and it lets us know that you've done your homework.

5
THE SUBMISSION PROCESS

Submitting your work for publication can be a daunting task and it would be easy to get bogged down by all of the details. Don't lose hope! Here's a simple checklist to ensure that you've covered all the bases:

1) My book is complete.
2) I have done an online search for publishers who specialize in my genre of book.
3) I have found the name and contact information of the person that I need to query.
4) I have read the submission guidelines for the publisher I have chosen and have completed all the expectations.
5) I have perfected my query letter.
6) I have perfected my synopsis.
7) My submission includes my contact information including email and phone number.
8) I have a professional email address where the publisher can reach me. (I can't stress this enough! I've seen some pretty scandalous ones in my time-yikes!)

You've completed the above checklist and now you're ready to submit your work to the publisher of your choice. You've double and triple checked to make sure that you're following the guidelines, and everything looks good. You press send and off it goes into cyberspace. Now what happens?

1) The publisher will **receive** your submission.
2) They will **read** your query and synopsis.
3) They will **decide** if they want more information and will check their roster for upcoming publications as to not duplicate ideas. If all is well, they will ask you for the first 5-10 pages of your manuscript (if it's a novel), or for your entire manuscript (if it's a children's book).
4) You will **send** them what they have requested.
5) They will read the **additional pages** and decide if your book is something that they'd like to see more of.
6) The publisher reader either **rejects or accepts** additional pages of the manuscript in its entirety.
7) **They send out a form rejection letter or a letter of acceptance.**
8) If it's a letter of acceptance the **contract** comes next.
9) If it's a letter of rejection, nothing happens. You **move on** to the next publisher.

The above process can take anywhere from 4-8 weeks to complete, sometimes longer, depending on the publisher and the circumstances.

DO NOT:

1) **Call or email the publisher** to check the status of your manuscript. We are very busy, but we promise we'll get to it. *If the publisher has directed you to follow up with them if you have not received a response within a specified window, go ahead and send them an email to check in.

2) **Expect any constructive criticism** or details as to why your work was rejected or things you can improve. The reason publishers use form rejection letters is because we are short on time, we aren't trying to be impersonal. Because we receive so many submissions each month, it's impossible for us to keep up and critique/offer guidance on what changes your manuscript needs.

3) **Resend your submission**. You will get confirmation from the publisher saying that they have received your submission.

4) **Get angry or abusive** with us if we reject your work. Conduct yourself with integrity and respect. A *no* now, doesn't always mean *no* forever.

5) **Give up**. Keep writing and keep sharpening your submission skills.

6) **Get down on yourself**. I mentioned before that I have enough rejection letters to wallpaper the side of my house! Don't lose hope, you'll get there eventually if you only keep trying and keep improving.

Insider Secret: Keep your email short and sweet. Let your query and synopsis do the talking! Publishers appreciate patience and we read every submission. To make your submission stand out, tell us something about ourselves or compare your book to one of ours! This allows us to cut to the chase and make a snap judgement if we want to see more of your work because now, we have something (that we know well) to measure against.

6
REASONS FOR REJECTION

Can you remember all the times you've been rejected? Maybe it was from that special someone that you had a grade school crush on, or perhaps it was being passed over for a promotion at your company. The fact is rejection is a part of life. Yes, it hurts and sometimes the scars of being rejected can last a lifetime. The same is true for publishing, but as scary as publishers can be sometimes, their opinion of your work is just that, their *opinion*. Yes, we are experts in our field but there are so many reasons for rejection that are not personal, so please don't give up!

Let's look at the five most common reasons for rejection from a publisher:

Reasons for Rejection:

1) **Not following the submission guidelines.** This will earn you an automatic disqualification, because how could we possibly move forward with you if you won't follow the rules?

2) **No room in the House.** Sometimes you have a great idea for a book, but so does someone else and they've beaten you to the punch. Publishers can only publish a certain amount of titles per year because time and investments are finite. Also, we could be at capacity for our children's titles that year or for our sci-fi offering. Occasionally, rejections are a matter of having a full roster.

3) **It's bad.** The manuscript is just plain bad and will cost too much money, time, or effort to repair. This is not limited to grammatical errors and hard to follow/dull plot lines, but sometimes it's about the content. We don't publish things that are inappropriate for the marketplace and if your work pushes the envelope too far, or is too controversial, we will reject you. Your work must be saleable because publishing is a business.

4) **Your social media profile is less than charming or non-existent.** Publishers are employers so you'd better believe that we Google you and check your online profiles to see if you align with our brand and our vision. You are a direct extension of us, and we prefer not to be embarrassed about who we choose to hire as authors to represent us. If you don't have a social media profile, publishers are wary of this because that means that you don't already have a platform set up with which to engage your potential readers. Author platforms take time to build and if you don't' have an established social media presence, it's more work for us.

5) **You've got a bad attitude/conflict of personality.** Because I'm a boutique publisher, I have the luxury of meeting my potential authors face to face. The reason I'm so grateful for this, is

because I get to gauge their personality and see if they are a good fit for my team. Not often, I've come across potential authors who are insufferably arrogant, unkind, racist, sexist, and just plain mean. Those are not the types of people that I mesh with and they're not the kind of people that I want in my House.

Insider Secret: Start your social media profile as soon as possible! Be sure to keep it clean and don't post anything that could lead to trouble in the future. Publishers also LOVE to see engagement with your audience/followers because this shows us that you'll be able to do the same with your readers. We also love working with people who are upbeat and have a positive attitude and excellent work ethic. Sometimes I've accepted manuscripts based on the author's merits and wonderful personality at the cost of cleaning up their less than stellar manuscript. We can work with potential!

7
SAMPLES

The best way to learn for most people is through examples and samples of things. Here is a sample of an excellent query letter, the **bolded sections** are what caught my attention:

Dear **Ms. Bakker,**

I see on your **company's website that you are currently searching for middle-grade fiction,** so I'm happy to introduce my novel titled, **Shards of Glass,** which won me a **scholarship** to a continuing education seminar in London with the **Society of Authors in the United Kingdom.**

Shards of Glass is about a fifteen-year-old girl named Harper Price who has run away from home because of the impending divorce between her bitter parents.

Her sister has accepted the divorce, but Harper can't help but feel betrayed by the people that professed to

love her most. **Determined to do whatever it takes to get her parents back together; Harper crafts a dangerous plan that will push her to the edge of her mental and physical limits. Just as she sets off on her journey, she is kidnapped by men she's met before, men who work with her father.**

The story is set in **New York City** and runs around **40,000** words. It's **similar in tone** to When He Vanished by T.J. Brearton.

I'm **a member of** the Society of Children's Book Writers and Illustrators and a member of Sisters in Crime.

Thank you for your consideration and I have included the first five pages of my manuscript **as requested.**

Sincerely,

Catherine Walker
(Contact information)

Let's review an example of a bad query letter:

To **whom it may concern,**

Please find my manuscript **attached**. My name is Catherine and I've written a story about a girl who is kidnapped by her father's staff.

She is crossing the street one night, and they take her. She tries to get away, but she can't, and she attempts to escape but doesn't succeed. My **family and friends really love**

my book and I think it's comparable to The **Hunger Games, but probably better**. Thanks for taking the time to read this, I hope you like it as much as I've liked writing it.

Catherine Walker

It's easy to see the difference between a good and bad query letter! The information is disorganized and there is no contact information. The genre is missing and so is the word count. She did not address the query letter to the person in charge, and her tone was very unprofessional. She also said that her friends and family loved the book and mentioned that her work was better than The Hunger Games. There is so much wrong with this version! Plus, she attached her entire manuscript and there was no mention of a title.

Let's look at an example of a good synopsis, I think you've heard this story before:

Cinderella is a young girl when her mother dies, and her father remarries a jealous woman with two horrible daughters. When Cinderella's father dies, her stepmother and stepsisters treat her like a slave. Her only friends are mice and she is banished to the attic bedroom and dreams of finding love and escaping the home and circumstances in which she lives.

The king who rules the kingdom that Cinderella lives in has a son who is set to be wed so that the king can meet his grandchildren before he passes away. The king decides to throw a royal ball and orders that all of the eligible young women in the kingdom must attend.

Cinderella is excited and she enlists the help of her animal friends to create a dress for her. But her stepmother and stepsisters destroy the dress before Cinderella is able to leave the house for the ball. She runs to the garden and cries when suddenly, her fairy godmother appears before her.

Cinderella can't believe her eyes as her fairy godmother creates a new, beautiful gown for her and turns a pumpkin into a golden carriage. Her godmother reminds her that she must be home by the stroke of midnight before the magic disappears and things return to normal.

Cinderella finally makes it to the royal ball and dances with the prince, the clock strikes midnight and she flees the steps of the royal castle to return home. In doing so, she loses a shoe.

The prince travels throughout the kingdom to find the lady who fits into the glass slipper. Cinderella's stepmother locks her in the attic, but her mice friends help her escape. She puts on the shoe and it's a perfect fit! Cinderella and her prince live happily ever after.

Here is an example of a bad synopsis:

Cinderella lives with her stepmother and stepsisters. They're mean to her and they won't let her attend a ball. Cinderella gets upset and cries in the garden. Her fairy godmother appears and makes her a dress and a carriage. Cinderella goes to the ball and loses a shoe. The price finds her, and they live happily ever after.

There is a huge difference not only in word count, but in the organization of information and the inclusion of plot points, climax, and conflict resolution.

Insider Secret: It's easier to cut back on a too long synopsis than it is to add to a too short synopsis. Give a detailed, yet general overview focusing mainly on plot points, climax, and conflict resolution. Publishers want to see a clear "big picture" version of your manuscript. Think of your synopsis as a book report. Be sure to review chapters 2 and 3 of this book for the proper way to write queries and synopsis.

8
MANUSCRIPT MISTAKES

Of course, there are hundreds of manuscript mistakes that we could talk about and this is by no means a complete list. However, they are the most frequent and most common mistakes we see as publishers when we review manuscripts.

1) **Over writing.** Whether it's being wordy or over explaining, it's important to keep things tight. Don't use eight words when four will do, and don't use anything more than, said, too often.

2) **Not using proper dialogue or dialogue is not believable.** Listen to a conversation between friends, notice how they speak. People use contractions and slang in everyday conversation with each other. Usually the tone is not formal, but more relaxed and casual. Obviously, it depends on the type of book you're writing for the level of formality needed in your dialogue.

3) **Getting the word count wrong for the genre.** Each genre has a very specific word count that publisher's live by. Children's books should not exceed 1,000 words, for example, but the sweet spot is between the 500 -800-word mark. There is a

method to our madness, and these are industry standards that you must know and abide by.

4) **Telling instead of showing.** Don't tell me that the moon was full, show me how it drips off a piece of broken glass in an abandoned parking lot in the middle of the night.

5) **Depending too much on the editor.** Don't be sloppy and don't just depend on editing tools that can't decipher tone and meaning. Editing is a much-needed human touch business, in order to convey the right message. Clean up your manuscript and don't leave things like common mistakes such as missing capitalization, missing quotations, and commas.

6) **Writing only one draft.** You should have a minimum of three drafts for your manuscript before you should even consider sending it in for potential publication and there should be enough time between draft and edits that you can look at your manuscript with fresh eyes.

7) **Switching tenses throughout your manuscript.** This happens so much and its very time consuming for editors to fix. Here's an example: She **looked (past tense)** out the window into the night and sighed, it **was** time for bed. She **sleeps** in and then she **makes (present tense)** coffee and **sits** by the window again.

Insider Secret: You double your chances of getting a book deal if your manuscript is concise and clean. Sometimes it pays to invest in an editor before sending your work into a publisher for consideration! We appreciate seeing a beautifully edited manuscript that needs little work because we see them so rarely! Hiring an editor will certainly make an impression and it will start you off on the right foot.

If you'd like to hire one of our professional editors, please click on the links below for more information:

https://pandamoniumpublishing.com/product/picture-book-line-editing/

https://pandamoniumpublishing.com/product/novel-editing-20000-55000-words/

https://pandamoniumpublishing.com/product/novel-editing-56000-to-79999-words/

https://pandamoniumpublishing.com/product/novel-editing-80000-to-89999-words/

https://pandamoniumpublishing.com/product/novel-editing-90000-to-10000-words/

9
WHAT PUBLISHERS WANT

So, I'll tell you what we want, what we really really want. We aren't complicated and we aren't asking too much of you. If you're dedicated to doing the things on this list, it's only a matter of time before you end up with a book deal.

1) **We want to be addressed properly.** We're real people whether you believe it or not, so please be kind. Please find out our names and address your correspondence accordingly. We aren't just a number or *to whom it may concern*. It's also a bonus if you can tell us why you chose us to submit your work to. We like to know that you've done your research because this means you're working with intention. Please always be respectful and don't take rejection personally.

2) **Have a positive attitude.** You can't have a great writing career if you don't think great thoughts. Your mindset is so important, and a positive outlook will help you sometimes more that skill ever could. Keep trying and if you fail, fail forward, learn from your

mistakes and become a better writer.

3) **Be willing to do the work.** Being an author isn't easy and publishers are looking for people who are going to work hard. Whether it's attending book signings or events, finishing edits and revisions on time, or a whole host of other things that we expect from you. The last thing we want to see is lack of effort or laziness on your part. We've invested a lot of money into your project and we want at least sweat equity in return.

4) **We want great stories and fresh, exciting points of view.** Can you tell a story from a different perspective? Did you put a new spin on an old character? Have you created a plot line that's intriguing and invigorating? Have you given your characters a new voice? We want things that haven't been done before!

5) **Communication skills are key.** From the very first time you send us an email to how you work as a member of our team is imperative. Lack of communication is the cause of all breakdowns in partnerships and contracts. If you're not able to communicate your book to us with a few sentences (elevator pitch), you'll never be able to sell us on it.

6) **Keep trying.** Don't give up! If you want to be a writer, then be a writer. Do the necessary things to become a more experienced and more articulate writer. Take classes, find beta groups, join clubs, and get honest feedback from professionals.

7) **Learn from your mistakes and continue to learn and expand on your knowledge.** I don't know an author out there who doesn't look back on their first manuscript and cringe. We *all* do it. But what's important is that we progress and become better

than we were in the last book.

8) **Read as much as you can.** Read things in your genre and things that are totally opposite of what you usually read. This expands our voices and our minds as writers and makes us stronger overall storytellers. Publishers can always tell by a manuscript who the avid readers are and who aren't.

10
FREQUENTLY ASKED QUESTIONS

I get on average 50 emails per week from authors asking for advice. Here are some of the best questions that I've answered over the years.

Q: "Lacey, how do you manage to keep positive when people tell you they don't like your work? I wrote a short story and my colleagues didn't care for it. They were nice enough, but I could tell that they weren't being completely truthful, so I pressed them, and they told me the truth finally. I was pretty upset and hurt. Maybe I should quit writing..."

A: This is a good question! I get hate mail all the time telling me that I'm a terrible writer, that people don't like my books, and that I should stop writing because I have no talent. It's something that comes with the territory and this business has given me a thick skin! Here's how I manage to stay positive:

1. **I remember that everyone is entitled to their opinion.** That's just it, it's their opinion and not the truth or reality that I choose to focus on. They can hate me and my books and I'm ok with it because writing is art and art is subjective.

2. **I stay in my own lane and focus on my own craft.** I don't pay attention to what other people say about me. You will never be criticized by someone doing more than you. Read that again. If I worried about what other people thought of me, I'd never write another word.

Q: "Lacey, I've written a book about the history of baseball and want to use photographs throughout my book, what do I need to know and is this possible?"

A: Great question! This whole copyrighting issue can get a bit messy at times, so let me explain how it works when wanting to use images.

1. **Stock Images**: You can use stock images that have no attribution required. There are multiple sites online that have stock images that you can use however you'd like. No attribution required means that you don't have to give credit to the photographer or the owner of the image.
2. **Public Domain**: Did you know that all images published before January 1, 1923, in the United States are now public domain? See if the images you'd like to use are in this category, because you may not need to get permission to use them.
3. **Buy Photos**: You can always buy photos from the photographer on sites like istockphoto.com, Shutterstock, and Fotosearch.
4. **Email**: Send an email to the person who holds the copyright of the image and ask their permission to use it. Sometimes there will be a charge and sometimes there won't it depend on what the owner of the photo decides.
5. **Wikipedia**: You can use the images from Wikipedia as long as you cite them.

In all cases, except for the first two on the list, you must give credit to the person who owns the photos. Please remember that copyright is very important and not something to be infringed upon. All artists deserve to be recognized for their work. It's up to them to say no attribution required, so always check beforehand what the case is. You'll save yourself a lot of trouble this way and be able to give credit where it is due.

Q: "Lacey, my family doesn't support my dream of becoming a writer. They tell me that I won't make any money and that I should focus on getting a real job. Writing is something I love, but I understand that I will need to pay my bills at the same time. How do I convince them that I'm doing something that I love and that this will pay off?"

A: Whoa...for a second after reading this, I was at a loss for words. I'll break it down because there are a couple of hidden questions in here and I don't want to miss them.

1. **My family doesn't support my dream of becoming a writer.** Sometimes, families aren't supportive of our dreams. They mean well, but then again, some of them don't. Some families don't support the arts, and they don't understand or appreciate any form of artistic expression. This can be very difficult. You have to follow your OWN path and whatever journey that leads you on. No one can decide what you should do with your life. If you want to be a writer, by all means, do it! Find others that will support you in *all* your endeavours no matter what they are.

2. **They tell me I won't make any money and I should focus on getting a real job.** I can tell you from first-hand experience that this has been said to me time and time again. "Writer's don't make any money," "How are you going to pay your bills?" "No one is going to buy your books," "Who do you think you are?" Yep, it hurts. But that's what makes victory so sweet. The fact is,

there are millions of writers out there who make plenty of money writing books. And there are so many ways to make a living writing! You can write for magazines, you can do copywriting, editing, content creation, blogging, journalism, and hundreds of other things that revolve around writing. Focus on honing your skills and getting as much experience as possible. Last time I checked, which was 56 seconds ago, writing was a real job.

3. **How can I convince them that I'm doing something I love and that this will pay off?** You can't and you never will convince them so stop trying. Do what you want to do because YOU want to do it. Life is way too short to be living your life based on what other people want you to do, say, or think. Getting up in the morning is a gamble, crossing the street is a gamble, travelling is a gamble, and the list goes on. There are no guarantees in life except that we only have one shot at it. Don't spend your life wondering *what if.* If this is what you want to do, you don't need anyone else's approval. I can't tell you that this will pay off, but what I can tell you is that you won't regret trying. We only regret the chances we never take.

Keep your head up. If you don't believe in yourself, who will?

Q: "Lacey, I don't read a lot of books because I don't have tons of time, I know you've said in the past that reading directly influences writing, so I'm wondering what I can do to make more time to read! Any suggestions?"

A: Ah, yes. This is a huge problem in society at the moment! We are living in such a fast-paced world that we barely have time to do anything pleasurable or just for fun. But making time to read is essential! Not only does reading lend to our ability to write, but it also makes us better writers, better storytellers, and more empathetic toward our fellow humans. The average Canadian adult has approximately 5 minutes per day to read! That's it. I admire your commitment to reading more and I'm so happy to help! Here's how I squeeze in time to read:

1) **I wake up an hour earlier or go to bed an hour later.** Carving out this hour to read is essential to my happiness and to my business as I usually read things that are relevant in my field such as trade magazines or what's trending on the best seller's list. This hour before or after allows me to be uninterrupted.

2) **I listen to audiobooks.** Audiobooks are portable and you can listen to them everywhere. I travel a lot, so this format of book allows me to get my reading done in the truck, on a plane, in the airport, on the treadmill, or wherever else I am. You wouldn't believe how much time is wasted while travelling and waiting!

3)**I read novellas, short stories, poems, and magazine articles.** Reading anything is better than not reading anything at all! I'll pick up a book shot by James Patterson for a quick, action-packed read that satisfies my craving for a good story in a short time.

 Q: "Lacey, as a writer how do you keep yourself from getting overwhelmed? How can you possibly stay organized with all of the books and projects you have?"

A: There are certainly days where I feel overwhelmed at times, but then I take a deep breath, remind myself that nothing is a crisis that can't be handled, and I immediately stop what I'm doing to do something else. It's very important that when you start to feel the walls closing in on you, that you change **anything.** Change your space, change your position in the room, stand up if you're sitting, get a fresh perspective and stop what you're working on! This is your brain's way of telling you that you need a few minutes to regroup. Take as much time as you need, take the afternoon off, go do something wild or out of your comfort zone, do whatever it takes to make sure that you're **ok**. You can't be any good to yourself or anyone else if you're burnt out and uninspired. It is ok to rest, it's ok to let go, it's ok to shut off your devices. It's essential to your wellbeing every once in a while to just be.

I'd be lying if I didn't say that I have pretty amazing systems in place that take a lot of the pressure off. I have a social media scheduler that allows me to plan my posts for 30 days at a time, I've got a dry erase calendar in my kitchen that has all of my things to do for the week in order of importance, and I use technology to streamline as many processes as possible such as pre-planning my blog posts and YouTube videos. If I had to post every day without this help, it would be near impossible to do so and would be a time-consuming pain.

Q: "Lacey, I've set goals for myself as writer and I've reached a few of them. I really want to be a famous author, but I can't stay on track no matter how hard I try. Should I throw in the towel and do something else with my life?"

A: Whoa, this question is deep; first of all, congratulations on reaching some of your goals, you've proven that it can be done and if you've done it once, you can certainly do it again! I'm a firm believer in never giving up no matter what and I know that some of you reading this will say it's easier said than done. But, if we all gave up when things got hard, none of us would accomplish anything. Today, I'm not going to talk about tips to stay disciplined or organized in your writing routine, nor will I give you my opinion on what you should and shouldn't do with your life because frankly, it doesn't matter what I think. I'm going to dive into the WHY part with a super simple exercise.

It's called 7 Whys… (I ended up calling the person who sent me this question and went through this with him, with his permission, I've posted his actual answers and he definitely gained clarity).

1. Start with a statement of what you want for your life: **I really want to be a famous author.**
2. **Why** do you want to be a famous author? Because I want people to read what I have to say.
3. **Why** do you want people to read what you have to say? Because what I have to say is important and I want to make lots of money at the same time.
4. **Why** is what you have to say important and why do you want to be rich? Because I'm tired of being silenced and not respected by friends and family and I'm tired of just being barely able to pay my bills.
5. **Why** are you tired of being silenced and not respected by friends and family, why are you tired of barely being able to pay your bills? Because they look down on me, I don't have as much education as them and they think my opinion and voice doesn't matter. Because I want to control my life and I don't want to make decisions based on how much money I do or don't have, ever again.
6. **Why** do they think your opinion and voice doesn't matter and why do you want to be in control of your life? Because I've never stood up for myself before, I usually just go along with whatever they say. I want to be in control because I'm sick of being controlled and decided for.
7. **Why** do you go along with whatever they say, why are you sick of being decided for and controlled? Because I don't trust myself and because I don't believe in my own capabilities. I'm sick of being controlled because I know that I can do better and that I can make better decisions. I want my family to stop being ashamed of me and I want to make them proud, I want to make myself proud.
8. **Why** do you want to make yourself and your family proud? Because I know that I can do better than I currently am. I'm just as able as my brothers and sisters to make something of myself.

I honestly felt like crying after this conversation. It was difficult for him to answer the questions, but he tells me he's glad he did.

So, in essence, this person wanted to be a writer because he wants to make himself and his family proud and he wants to make something of himself and his life. This is his ultimate reason for writing and when the dark days come, he can look at his reason **why** and keep going. The other reasons before this one was superficial at best. They wouldn't be enough to keep him on track.

Wow...we dug deep, didn't we? The point of the exercise is during the first few whys, the brain gives a nice, neat, acceptable answer, but after the 5th why, it starts to get subconscious. Write down what you want and ask yourself why 7 times, building on the previous answer. Don't go any further. You have your reason to continue or your reason to quit.

Q: "Lacey, you have a ton of content on your site, how do you think of fresh ideas all of the time?"

A: Thank you for noticing first of all! I try so hard to bring fresh ideas and new things for us to talk about! Some days it can be a struggle that's for sure, especially when we have a blog, YouTube channel, podcast, and various social media to keep up with. I do my best not to duplicate content, so you won't get a podcast that has the same info or material as on our blog, etc. When it comes to finding inspiration for content, here's what I do:

1. **I scour the news.** Yep, it's depressing at times, but I look for things that I can talk or write about especially when it comes to creative writing. Sometimes the headlines can inspire a book idea or a skewed perspective for a topic that I can share.

2. **I listen to conversations.** Eavesdropping? Check. When I'm out getting coffee or I'm shopping, or anywhere in public, I listen to the people around me. Sometimes waiting in line at a place can provide lots of great ideas!
3. **I read trade publications like Writer's Digest and subscribe to magazines in my field of work.** This allows for a lot of ideas on topics that are relevant for our readers and writers who visit and subscribe to our content. It also means that staying up to date on all things publishing is essential in bringing the most relevant topics to our media.

Q: "Lacey, I'm working on a couple of novels at the same time and I'm having a hard time keeping things straight! I've mixed up my characters and plots in a couple of points during the story and am driving myself crazy. How do I fix this?"

A: Well, kudos to you for working on not one, but two novels! That's very exciting. Yes, it can be difficult when working on multiple projects to keep things in order. I can't tell you how many manuscripts I've edited that have had the wrong name (or the previous name) of the character written down in later chapters. The good news is that it happens to everyone. The other good news is that it's easy to fix!

1. **Sticky notes are your friend.** Before sitting down to work on either one of your novels take a sticky note and write the main character's name in BOLD, BLACK, marker. Stick it to the screen of your laptop. This is a visual reminder of what you're working on and which character/book requires your attention.
2. **One thing per day.** Section your week into specific days that you will work on each project. For example, I write Becoming James Cass on Monday, Tuesday, and Wednesday, and I write I am Jessica Westlake on Thursday, Friday, and Saturday. It's much easier to

write on certain days rather than to spend the morning of each day working on project one, and the afternoon working on project two. You'll be less inclined to make a mistake...unless of course you're like me and you never know what day it is.

Q: "Lacey, when should I send my novel to a publisher for consideration?"

A: There are a few things that you need to keep in mind for submitting your work to a publisher.

1. **AFTER** your manuscript is completed.
2. **AFTER** you do your research (see who is accepting manuscripts and if that publisher is accepting your genre)
3. **AFTER** you query the publisher and they REQUEST your manuscript. Your query better be good by the way.

"But Lacey, why wouldn't I query first to see if they're even interested? Then if they are, I'll finish my book."

Think of it this way, you send us a killer query letter, we love it, and want to see the manuscript, imagine our disdain if your manuscript is unfinished. You've completely wasted your time and ours. This is comparable to a real estate agent saying to you, "I've found your dream home! It's got everything you want, a pool, a big backyard, and three car garage!" You're excited, right? Then she says, "But it's not for sale." That's how publishers feel when you tell us the manuscript is incomplete. Don't ever do this, make sure your work is finished before ever considering querying us.

"But Lacey, can't I just send my book out to a bunch of publishers to better my chances?"

No. Next question. Just kidding; all kidding aside though, you need to research the publisher that is the best fit for your work. Let's say that you wrote a middle-grade adventure novel and you sent your manuscript to a publisher who only publishes romantic fiction for adults...again, you've wasted your time and ours. Do your research, know who you are submitting to, and know what they publish. If you submit something to us that is totally out of our scope, we realize that not only did you NOT do your research but maybe you don't care enough about a book deal to do your homework. It also makes us leery of working with you because you've shown us that you can't follow instructions.

"But Lacey, can't I include my manuscript with the query? It will be more efficient, and I won't have to wait as long for a response."

Do NOT send your manuscript with the query. If we want it, we'll ask for it. You also need to be aware of the guidelines. A lot of the time publishers request the first 5-10 pages of your manuscript in the BODY of the email. We don't open attachments so if you've ignored the guidelines and sent us your query and manuscript together...you may as well consider it trashed because we won't open it.

I know that a lot of this advice seems a bit harsh, but this is the reality of publishing. I want you to have your best shot at success.

Q: "Lacey, I've written a picture book and I keep getting rejected! One publisher told me that my manuscript was boring...I don't know what to do, please help!"

A: Ouch. Let me just say that at least this person got a response back from a publisher that wasn't just a form letter and now the writer can regroup and start again. The publisher isn't being a jerk because they want to be, they're just sick and tired of the same old, same old. Let me explain what publisher's DON'T WANT to see in Kid's books.

1. **They don't want the same old characters**. Diversity is key. We want to see characters that have different backgrounds, different beliefs, and celebrations, that have different abilities, different family units, and different ethnicities. Kids want to see books on the shelves that look like them! They can't be what they can't see.

2. **They don't want the same old story**. Done to death is an expression that I use more often than I'd like to. We are tired of the same old stories that sound like this, "Timmy went to school and had a nice day. His teacher was nice, he made friends and came home. He couldn't wait to go to school the next day. The End." Someone please hand me a sharp object so that I can gouge my eyes out. Look at books that are unique and different a la The Day The Crayons Quit, or The Book With No Pictures, or P is for Pterodactyl. (Three of my favourites that I wish I had written, insert crying face here.)

3. **They don't want something that won't sell.** Saleability is key. A picture book is around an $8,000.00 investment for the publisher. We want to at least make our money back and then some. Don't send us a book that preaches to kids (leave that to the parents) or that is the fifteenth of its kind (e.g. Diary of a Not So Wimpy Kid...also a legal liability) or that is not marketable. I'll leave the politics and religion out of this, but I know you get the drift.

Those are just three things we don't want to see on our desk as publishers. There are more, but if you stick to leaving these out, you'll have a good shot at getting your manuscript read

Q: "Lacey, is it hard being an author?"

A: Yes. Next question. Ok, but seriously, yes-it's extremely difficult to not only become an author but to stay an author. Let me explain the rollercoaster:

1. **Beginning:** You'll be rejected more times that you can count. You will think you're a no-talent hack and that's on the good days. You'll cry yourself to sleep and then wake up the next morning and do it all over again. You'll suffer from insomnia and find yourself asking, WHAT THE F*CK *at least* once a day when your characters refuse to speak to you.

2. **Middle:** You'll finally get a book deal and be on top of the world! You'll feel like you've made it, but now the work truly begins. You worry about the next book and what if the publisher hates it, what if you're a one-hit wonder, what if people hate your book? You'll feel totally vulnerable and second guess every single word you write. The waiting is the worst part as it usually takes 2-5 years for a book to be released to the public. You'll want to throw in the towel but don't! You still have to fight with your editor and publisher when they recommend taking out the best part of your story.

3. **End:** Your book comes out and now your work has increased four hundredfold. You have to market the book, (yes, even if you're traditionally published), sell the book, talk to people about the book, set up your displays, network, make contacts, do book signings, lug your crap from place to place and sweat your ass off while doing it in 5 inch stilettos. You'll have people tell you to your face that they don't like your work or even better, that they don't like you. Some days you'll go home with your tail between your legs because you didn't sell a single copy of your book even though you tried with all of your might.

But listen, it's not all bad. Being an author has been one of the most rewarding experiences of my life. And the icing on the cake? Reading my nephews and niece the books that I WROTE and dedicated to them. You'll make friends with amazing people and those friendships last for life. You'll have fabulous opportunities around the world to talk about your books and visit international book fairs in various countries. You'll be asked to be a guest speaker at major events, and you'll get to read your book to kids in schools all over the city and the country. People will find your books on the shelf at major stores and around the world. Your books make a difference and one day, someone will tell you that YOU are their favourite author. The GOOD outweighs whatever bad there is. The world needs your art so go out there and create something that outlives you.

I hope that you've enjoyed this book! If you would like to leave a review on Amazon, I would appreciate it very much. Thanks for reading, until next time, keep writing because your words have the power to change the world.

X LLB

ABOUT THE AUTHOR

Lacey L. Bakker is the owner of Pandamonium Publishing House in Hamilton, Ontario, Canada. She founded the boutique publishing company in 2015 and named it after her first children's book (and real-life cat), Panda the Very Bad Cat. She has been published internationally in various publications such as Chicken Soup for the Soul, and Women's World Magazine, over a dozen times. She is the author of twenty books and counting and writes for children under her current name, and for adults under her pen name of L.L. Colling. She has been featured on blogs, podcasts, newsletters, seminars, and workshops as a guest speaker. Lacey has been nominated for Best Local Author and she is an avid fan of hockey and baseball. She enjoys spending time with her best friend, Simba, traveling the world, and reading.

www.pandamoniumpublishing.com

Facebook: Pandamonium Publishing House

Instagram: Lacey L. Bakker

Twitter: Laceybakker1

To subscribe to our newsletter email us at
pandapublishing8@gmail.com

www.ingramcontent.com/pod-product-compliance
Lightning Source LLC
Chambersburg PA
CBHW032121280326
41933CB00009B/939